ROMARE
BEARDEN

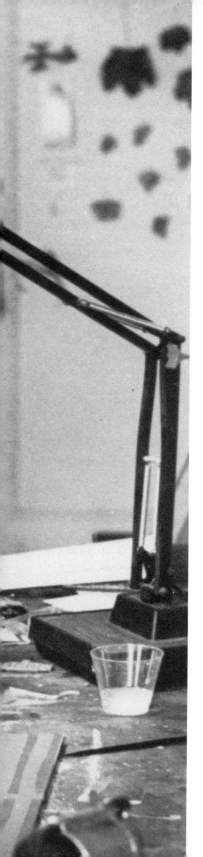

ROMARE BEARDEN

Kevin Brown

CHELSEA HOUSE PUBLISHERS

New York   Philadelphia

Chelsea House Publishers
Editorial Director Richard Rennert
Executive Managing Editor Karyn Gullen Browne
Copy Chief Robin James
Picture Editor Adrian G. Allen
Art Director Robert Mitchell
Manufacturing Director Gerald Levine
Assistant Art Director Joan Ferrigno

Black Americans of Achievement
Senior Editors Sean Dolan, Philip Koslow

Staff for ROMARE BEARDEN
Editorial Assistants Annie McDonnell, Sydra Mallery
Designer John Infantino
Picture Researcher Ellen Barrett Dudley
Cover Illustrator Michael Garland

3 5 7 9 8 6 4 2

Library of Congress Cataloging-in-Publication Data
Brown, Kevin, 1960–
  Romare Bearden/Kevin Brown
    p. cm.—(Black Americans of achievement)
  Includes bibliographical references and index.
    ISBN 0-7910-1119-4.
      0-7910-1145-3 (pbk.)
  1. Bearden, Romare, 1911–1988—Juvenile literature. 2. Afro-
American artists—Biography—Juvenile literature. [1. Bearden,
Romare, 1911–1988. 2. Artists. 3. Afro-Americans—Biography.] I.
Title. II. Series.
N6537.B4B76 1994   94-867
709'.2—dc20   CIP
[B]   AC

Frontispiece: *When working, Romare Bearden invariably wore blue coveralls and a soft felt cap. "There was a decidedly special aura about him," wrote his biographer Myron Schwartzman. "He was a man whose presence charged a room with intelligence."*

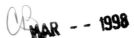

CONTENTS

BLACK AMERICANS OF ACHIEVEMENT

HENRY AARON
baseball great

KAREEM ABDUL-JABBAR
basketball great

RALPH ABERNATHY
civil rights leader

ALVIN AILEY
choreographer

MUHAMMAD ALI
heavyweight champion

RICHARD ALLEN
*religious leader and
social activist*

MAYA ANGELOU
author

LOUIS ARMSTRONG
musician

ARTHUR ASHE
tennis great

JOSEPHINE BAKER
entertainer

JAMES BALDWIN
author

BENJAMIN BANNEKER
scientist and mathematician

AMIRI BARAKA
poet and playwright

COUNT BASIE
bandleader and composer

ROMARE BEARDEN
artist

JAMES BECKWOURTH
frontiersman

MARY MCLEOD BETHUNE
educator

JULIAN BOND
civil rights leader and politician

GWENDOLYN BROOKS
poet

JIM BROWN
football great

RALPH BUNCHE
diplomat

STOKELY CARMICHAEL
civil rights leader

GEORGE WASHINGTON
CARVER
botanist

RAY CHARLES
musician

CHARLES CHESNUTT
author

JOHN COLTRANE
musician

BILL COSBY
entertainer

PAUL CUFFE
merchant and abolitionist

COUNTEE CULLEN
poet

BENJAMIN DAVIS, SR., AND
BENJAMIN DAVIS, JR.
military leaders

SAMMY DAVIS, JR.
entertainer

FATHER DIVINE
religious leader

FREDERICK DOUGLASS
abolitionist editor

CHARLES DREW
physician

W. E. B. DU BOIS
scholar and activist

PAUL LAURENCE DUNBAR
poet

KATHERINE DUNHAM
dancer and choreographer

DUKE ELLINGTON
bandleader and composer

RALPH ELLISON
author

JULIUS ERVING
basketball great

JAMES FARMER
civil rights leader

ELLA FITZGERALD
singer

MARCUS GARVEY
black nationalist leader

JOSH GIBSON
baseball great

DIZZY GILLESPIE
musician

WHOOPI GOLDBERG
entertainer

ALEX HALEY
author

PRINCE HALL
social reformer

MATTHEW HENSON
explorer

CHESTER HIMES
author

BILLIE HOLIDAY
singer

LENA HORNE
entertainer

LANGSTON HUGHES
poet

ZORA NEALE HURSTON
author

JESSE JACKSON
civil rights leader and politician

MICHAEL JACKSON
entertainer

JACK JOHNSON
heavyweight champion

JAMES WELDON JOHNSON
author

MAGIC JOHNSON
basketball great

SCOTT JOPLIN
composer

BARBARA JORDAN
politician

MICHAEL JORDAN
basketball great

CORETTA SCOTT KING
civil rights leader

MARTIN LUTHER KING, JR.
civil rights leader

LEWIS LATIMER
scientist

SPIKE LEE
filmmaker

CARL LEWIS
champion athlete

JOE LOUIS
heavyweight champion

RONALD MCNAIR
astronaut

MALCOLM X
militant black leader

THURGOOD MARSHALL
Supreme Court justice

TONI MORRISON
author

ELIJAH MUHAMMAD
religious leader

EDDIE MURPHY
entertainer

JESSE OWENS
champion athlete

SATCHEL PAIGE
baseball great

CHARLIE PARKER
musician

GORDON PARKS
photographer

ROSA PARKS
civil rights leader

SIDNEY POITIER
actor

ADAM CLAYTON
POWELL, JR.
political leader

COLIN POWELL
military leader

LEONTYNE PRICE
opera singer

A. PHILIP RANDOLPH
labor leader

PAUL ROBESON
singer and actor

JACKIE ROBINSON
baseball great

DIANA ROSS
entertainer

BILL RUSSELL
basketball great

JOHN RUSSWURM
publisher

SOJOURNER TRUTH
antislavery activist

HARRIET TUBMAN
antislavery activist

NAT TURNER
slave revolt leader

DENMARK VESEY
slave revolt leader

ALICE WALKER
author

MADAM C. J. WALKER
entrepreneur

BOOKER T. WASHINGTON
educator and racial spokesman

IDA WELLS-BARNETT
civil rights leader

WALTER WHITE
civil rights leader

OPRAH WINFREY
entertainer

STEVIE WONDER
musician

RICHARD WRIGHT
author

ON
ACHIEVEMENT

———— ❧ ————

Coretta Scott King

Bᴇғᴏʀᴇ ʏᴏᴜ ʙᴇɢɪɴ this book, I hope you will ask yourself what the word *excellence* means to you. I think that it's a question we should all ask, and keep asking as we grow older and change. Because the truest answer to it should never change. When you think of excellence, perhaps you think of success at work; or of becoming wealthy; or meeting the right person, getting married, and having a good family life.

Those important goals are worth striving for, but there is a better way to look at excellence. As Martin Luther King, Jr., said in one of his last sermons, "I want you to be first in love. I want you to be first in moral excellence. I want you to be first in generosity. If you want to be important, wonderful. If you want to be great, wonderful. But recognize that he who is greatest among you shall be your servant."

My husband, Martin Luther King, Jr., knew that the true meaning of achievement is service. When I met him, in 1952, he was already ordained as a Baptist preacher and was working toward a doctoral degree at Boston University. I was studying at the New England Conservatory and dreamed of accomplishments in music. We married a year later, and after I graduated the following year we moved to Montgomery, Alabama. We didn't know it then, but our notions of achievement were about to undergo a dramatic change.

You may have read or heard about what happened next. What began with the boycott of a local bus line grew into a national movement, and by the time he was assassinated in 1968 my husband had fashioned a black movement powerful enough to shatter forever the practice of racial segregation. What you may not have read about is where he got his method for resisting injustice without compromising his religious beliefs.

He adopted the strategy of nonviolence from a man of a different race, who lived in a different country, and even practiced a different religion. The man was Mahatma Gandhi, the great leader of India, who devoted his life to serving humanity in the spirit of love and nonviolence. It was in these principles that Martin discovered his method for social reform. More than anything else, those two principles were the key to his achievements.

This book is about black Americans who served society through the excellence of their achievements. It forms a part of the rich history of black men and women in America—a history of stunning accomplishments in every field of human endeavor, from literature and art to science, industry, education, diplomacy, athletics, jurisprudence, even polar exploration.

Not all of the people in this history had the same ideals, but I think you will find something that all of them had in common. Like Martin Luther King, Jr., they all decided to become "drum majors" and serve humanity. In that principle—whether it was expressed in books, inventions, or song—they found something outside themselves to use as a goal and a guide. Something that showed them a way to serve others, instead of only living for themselves.

Reading the stories of these courageous men and women not only helps us discover the principles that we will use to guide our own lives but also teaches us about our black heritage and about America itself. It is crucial for us to know the heroes and heroines of our history and to realize that the price we paid in our struggle for equality in America was dear. But we must also understand that we have gotten as far as we have partly because America's democratic system and ideals made it possible.

We are still struggling with racism and prejudice. But the great men and women in this series are a tribute to the spirit of our democratic ideals and the system in which they have flourished. And that makes their stories special and worth knowing. ❧

1

"TO REDEFINE THE IMAGE OF MAN"

ONE SPRING morning in 1964, the painter Romare Bearden was pacing back and forth in his New York studio. He had scheduled an afternoon appointment with the art dealer Arne Ekstrom, who handled his work. They were meeting to discuss ideas for an exhibition in the fall.

Bearden was thinking about his career. At 53, he was almost an old man. For more than 25 years he had divided himself between what he did for a living and what he lived for. Each day, he came home tired and often frustrated. Still, five—sometimes six—days a week, he painted without fail.

But not always with success. Though Ekstrom was an old friend, the hardest moment in any artist's life is when his or her soul is bared before another. The gamble is risky, at best. Each time, the stakes can seem like life or death. And Bearden felt that he had more riding on his newest batch of work than ever before.

Because the lighting in Bearden's loft was not good, spotlights were trained on the pictures that hung from the walls. There was a window at the front. He looked out and saw that it was overcast. Bearden was famous for the deep, rich colors in his work—fuchsias, magentas, imperial purples, and ultramarine blues—but he loved the color gray. For him, gray was the middle ground between the violence at either end of the spectrum, and the overcast skies seemed to speak to him about the proper place of his work in a society grappling, not always successfully, with weighty moral and political issues.

Outside, in the world beyond the view from his windows, racial and political violence were running riot in the streets. The country seemed as if it was being torn slowly apart. In the South the struggle of black Americans for an end to segregation, for voting rights, and for equal economic and educational opportunity was meeting with obfuscation, resistance, and outright violence; some even likened the situation to a new civil war. In the North the long-compressed rage of black Americans at the myriad inequities of the American system was smoldering, soon to explode in fiery rage. The assassinations a year earlier of President John F. Kennedy and civil rights leader Medgar Evers testified to the volatile state of the nation and its seemingly infinite capacity for violence. Thousands of miles away, the United States was becoming with each passing day more deeply committed to participation in Vietnam's civil war, an involvement that would ultimately become an even more divisive issue than the civil rights movement.

Though no sentimentalist, Bearden liked to think of his studio, like his palette, as a neutral zone. Art, he felt, could create righteous anger, but righteous anger alone could not create art. Not that he was in any way an escape artist. On the contrary, he thought of art as a great responsibility and "a proud career." However beautiful it might be, great art was never merely decorative. "I think the only way to escape from reality is to get to the heart of it; confronting it, moving to the core is the only way," he once said. His intention in his art was not to escape social responsibility, but to impose, in the solitude of his studio, some order and meaning upon the

senselessness of life in a chaotic world. "Every artist," he said, "must find something to set him free, and something he can set free."

Romare Bearden traveled in two different worlds—and they were worlds apart. He had been raised uptown in New York City, in Harlem, a predominantly black world of stoops and storefront churches. This was the world of his people. But he lived downtown, in Soho, near Greenwich Village. Mostly white, it was a world of galleries and cafés. This was the world of his friends.

As an African-American artist, Bearden was committed to portraying the life of his people. As an artist, he felt convinced that he must express that life in a way all people could understand. "And, to accomplish this, the Negro artist," he insisted, "must

In his relentless quest for artistic excellence, Bearden sought a way to represent the black American experience that would be as truthful as Pieter Breughel the Elder's paintings of Flemish peasant life in the 16th century. Reproduced here is Breughel's famous Netherlandish Proverbs.

come to think of himself not primarily as a Negro, but as an artist."

Bearden was a universalist. He believed that there is "only one art, and it belongs to all mankind." He wanted "to paint the life of my people as I know it—as passionately and dispassionately as Breughel painted the life of the Flemish people of his day."

This was his dilemma as an African-American artist. He wanted to make a statement, but on his own terms. He wanted to paint life, but according to the colors of his soul. And his soul was not simply black-and-white. His ambition—nothing less than heroic in his eyes—was "to redefine the image of man" in terms of the black experience.

He set about to paint. Workman that he was, he dressed in blue overalls. Art supplies were everywhere. Beside him were sheets of paper soaked in water. Paintbrushes, paper cuttings, paste, and scissors littered his worktable. In the studio Bearden was strictly a soloist. No one was allowed to watch him while he worked. If he was just drawing doodles, perhaps. But if he was painting, never.

The cats, of course, were free to do as they pleased. Gyppo stalked along the tops of canvases stacked against the wall. Michelangelo ("Mickey") was more inclined to lie on the worktable, pawing pencils gingerly. Their antics did not bother Bearden. He loved cats. In fact, he was something of a big cat himself: cautiously affectionate, intelligently sensual, discreetly bold, and cunningly sincere.

He worked in solitude, but not in silence. If art was his love, then music was his mistress. In the afternoons while he worked he listened to classical or jazz on the radio station of Columbia University. Romare Bearden was trained in mathematics, and music, he liked to think, is the sound of numbers singing. The mathematical graph of a curve, the logic and rigor of a musical phrase, the beauty and grace of a cat—these were a few of his favorite things.

From floor to ceiling, books by the thousands lined the shelves of his loft. Sometimes, searching for ideas, he sat poring over Japanese prints or old photographs from his native South. When he conceived of a subject, he would then envision a setting. The subject and the setting, to some extent, determined his choice of materials.

Bearden worked in many different media throughout his career. He started out with watercolor, a transparent, lightly textured paint. Next he tried tempera, a fast-drying, durable yolk-based pigment. Gradually, he moved to experimentation with oil and acrylic. Finally he found his home in collage.

Collage is a method of composition using paper, fabric, or other everyday materials pasted onto a background. Originating in the 19th century, collage as fine art was reinvented at the turn of the century by the likes of Georges Braque, Henri Matisse, and Pablo Picasso. Collage is much the same kind of composition with scissors, paper, and paste that kindergartners make, but in the hands of a master like Bearden, as he himself put it, collage is "not child's play but divine play." Collage is tricky; just the right glues and papers must be used or the work disintegrates. The art of collage was like life, Bearden felt: you took what you had and made the best of it.

Bearden rarely made a preliminary sketch. He began the actual painting with a background. First he laid down several small, canvas-shaped rectangles: frames within the frame. These he positioned up, down, and across the canvas. The idea was to create a balance between the horizontal and the vertical. Then, the background laid, he could experiment— just to see what would happen. In the same way, a jazz musician might establish a melody and key and

African-American music—particularly blues and jazz—served as a constant source of inspiration to Bearden, who sometimes likened his method of composition to that of a jazz instrumentalist: "You do something, and then you improvise." Among the jazz artists Bearden admired was the great trumpeter Miles Davis.

then improvise freely upon it. Bearden's style of composition was in keeping with this musical idea. This combination of freedom and structure was the essence of what he sometimes called his "visual jazz." "I like the language to be as classical as possible," he said, but it also had to seem completely spontaneous; it had to breathe; and it had, above all, to sing.

Bearden then pasted down precut shapes, smoothing them out with an ink roller. Working rapidly, he trusted to experience and instinct. He was now master of his medium and could invent his own rules. "Once you get going," he observed, "all sorts of things open up." On a good day it felt as if his head and hand were one. Sometimes things just seemed "to fall into place, like the piano keys that seem to be right where your fingers come down."

Always, unexpected combinations of scenes and characters would surprise him. Suddenly, out of the blue, there they were. No one knows just how this happens, least of all the artist. "If you work in an art," he explained, "it wants to help you. But you must follow where it leads." He wanted the thing to take on a life of its own. "I don't 'do' a collage," he explained. "I just allow some of the people I know to come into the room."

That was the awe-inspiring thing about the process. Art was infinite. No matter how much he knew, there was always more to learn. It could be mastered, but never perfected. Each work was unique and had a mind of its own. "Different times call for different solutions," he often said. As in mathematics, the trick was to find the right solution for a particular problem. "Art," he said, "is an adventure and a search."

It was not always smooth sailing. At first Bearden used canvas for his collages. But canvas breathes and warps. Sometimes he stretched a canvas so tight the backing snapped like a rubber band. And often, because he could not press hard enough, bubbles formed under the glued paper. An artist friend once showed him how to use Masonite board, which allowed him to prepaint his surfaces. But Masonite was too heavy for hanging very large collages and fell off the wall. Art is not magic. It is the result of years of hard work, trial, and error.

Finally there were the finishing touches. He applied several coats of lacquer in order to even out the color, smooth the surface, and ultimately protect the work. At the end of his working day he stepped back from what he had made and saw that it was good. It was finished. His work was done. But Bearden realized that knowing what he wanted to say was one thing. Making himself understood was quite another. Would Ekstrom understand?

Slowly, Arne Ekstrom trudged up the stairs at 357 Canal Street. At each floor, he stopped to catch his breath. These were easily the steepest five flights he had ever climbed.

Ekstrom was co-owner of Cordier & Ekstrom, an expensive space on Madison Avenue's "gallery row." Bearden and Ekstrom had met on a freezing day back in 1959. "Romie"—everybody called him that—had been recommended to "Mr. E" by a mutual friend.

In 1961 Ekstrom had given Romie a solo exhibition. Entitled *Cool Jazz,* it consisted of a series of untitled abstractions: colors, shapes, and patterns representing inner moods rather than recognizably external objects. Their muted tones and textures were the visual equivalent of the cool jazz pioneered by trumpeter Miles Davis. This exhibition had greatly impressed the art world, and Mr. E had scaled those stairs—they "rose to the sky," he said, "the worst stairs and the worst climb"—many times since. For the next 30 years Cordier & Ekstrom would be synonymous with Romare Bearden, and vice versa.

Romare's wife, Nanette, was busy in the kitchen at the rear of their long, narrow loft. She answered the door, smiled, and showed Mr. E in. Romie was right behind her. Mr. E thought marriage looked good on Romie. He seemed happier, healthier than he had in years.

On first meeting Romie few people realized he was black. At 5 feet 11 inches and 210 pounds, with light skin and hazel eyes, he looked if anything Russian. But when, as often happened, he threw back his big bald head and laughed with great gusto, friends said, his black ancestry was made clearly apparent. "Nobody but a Negro man is going to laugh like that," his friend, the writer Albert Murray, said.

After some small talk, Nanette went back into the kitchen. The two men went up front to the studio. Mr. E noticed the enormous artworks wrapped up and standing over against the wall. Pointing, he asked whether he might see them. At first Romie tried to change the subject. He felt they were too raw, too radical. But Mr. E insisted. Reluctantly, Romie gave in.

The powerful black-and-white images staggered Ekstrom. Cut-and-pasted assemblages of newspaper and magazine cuttings, these "photomontages" were unlike anything Bearden had ever done. They were a crowded portrait gallery of black faces and figures— part African mask, part animal eyes, part roots, leaves, twigs, vines, and other vegetation. They combined huge eyes with small faces, small bodies with huge hands. And they had strange, hypnotic names: *Evening, 9:10, 461 Lenox Avenue*; *Mysteries*; and *The Prevalence of Ritual*.

They were hard-edged, urban, riotous: joyful music, loud laughter, card playing, tenement windows open to the sounds of the summertime streets. Or they were lyrical, rural, serene: wooden shacks fronting on the cotton fields, children staring out in unblinking wonder, old black faces lined with pain, trains, birds in flight, and other "journeying things."

The themes to which Bearden had returned again and again throughout his career—the good earth, the beauty of black women, and the presence of the past—were all here. He had used the medium of collage to create unique works of art, analyze social and political issues, and tell his own story, all at the same time.

All the lessons learned in 50 years of living and looking had been successfully brought together. Here was all of African-American history—slavery, the rape of scattered tribes, emancipation, great

Bearden's art reached a new level of achievement with the collages he began to fashion in the early 1960s, such as The Prevalence of Ritual: Baptism.

migrations. Here was all of art history—Chinese painting, African sculpture, cubism, collage. And here as well was his whole personal history—his southern birth, his Pittsburgh boyhood, his Harlem manhood, his Paris exile and return. After decades of struggle, Bearden had finally found a vehicle worthy of his vision.

Ekstrom immediately saw that these quilted images of memory and metaphor were greater than the sum of their patchwork parts. Their seeming chaos of impressions—their distortions, dislocations, and relocations—was in fact a strictly ordered imitation of life. Their jumble of faces and features cast a whole new light on the complexion of the black experience.

He saw that, just as the moving camera shoots both far across and deep into the visual scene, these scissored images moved through both landscape and history, compressing space and time. Fixed and faded newspaper cuttings, torn and tattered fragments, these symbolic images represented a restless still-life documentary of African-American history.

But Ekstrom saw more than that. He saw that the collages were the artistically successful equivalent of that integration of political elements—many peoples, one nation—for which the people, even now, were marching in the streets. If you looked hard enough and thought deeply enough, they were a metaphor in black-and-white, for that greatest of migrations: the American experience.

Ekstrom had understood, all right. In fact, he was ecstatic. "That's your next show!" he cried. ✎

2

MEMORIES OF
MECKLENBURG COUNTY

FRED ROMARE HOWARD BEARDEN was born on Saturday, September 2, 1911, in Charlotte, North Carolina. "Most artists take some place, and like a flower, they sink roots," he said. "My roots are in North Carolina."

The artist's studio in Long Island City, New York, where he worked from 1967 until the end of his life, was a clean, well-lighted place. But it was austere. There was no telephone, no television, no distraction of any kind. The only sign of human attachment was an old photograph of a man and a woman.

Thin and light-complexioned, the man sits with one fist clenched. His finger is aimed pointedly at his dusty, well-worn shoes. His feet are firmly planted on the porch of his homestead. "This," he seems to say, "is mine. I've earned it. Nobody can take it from me." He is the portrait of proud determination.

By his side sits a woman in a floor-length dress. Her face, strong but worn, is like those that mysteriously reappear in Romare Bearden's photomontages half a century later. Her hands are folded in her lap. Dark and round and soft, she is the image of patience and gentleness.

Bearden himself was something of a storyteller. Yet this one picture, taped as if for inspiration to the wall just above his worktable, tells the story of his

Bearden always kept this photograph of his paternal great-grandparents H. B. and Rosa Kennedy in his work space as a source of inspiration.

H. B. and Rosa Kennedy flank six-year-old Romare Bearden. Standing behind them (from right) are Romare's aunt Anna; his mother, Bessye Johnson Banks Bearden; his father, Richard Howard Bearden; and his grandmother Cattie Kennedy Bearden.

life better than 20,000 words could do. The people in the photograph are Henry ("H. B.") and Rosa Gosprey Kennedy, Romare's paternal great-grandparents. Bearden's beginning was Bearden's end. If the North Carolina soil is the root, these two figures are the stem of his later flowering.

H. B. and Rosa started out as servants. In the 1860s they worked together in the household of Dr. Joseph Wilson in Columbia, South Carolina. The Wilsons' young son was then still living at home. Like one of the Beardens' own descendants, he would make his mark upon the world one day. In 1912, the year after Romare Bearden was born, Woodrow Wilson was elected the 28th president of the United States.

The years 1865–76 are referred to by historians as the Reconstruction era. In the aftermath of the Civil War, Congress enacted sweeping social and political reforms; the 14th and 15th amendments extended citizenship to blacks and guaranteed their civil rights. Like the civil rights era of the 1950s and 1960s, Reconstruction was a period of great progress and great expectations. H. B. and men like him exchanged the shackles of slavery for freedom and self-respect. Some even acquired political office. In a way, the nation Romare Bearden painted from his studio window 100 years later had been born then.

By now, H. B. had a family. He married young, at age 18, in 1863, and his daughter Catherine ("Cattie") was born at the close of the Civil War. In the 1870s he took his wife and child north to Charlotte. There he settled, worked hard as a mail agent for the Charlotte, Columbia and Augusta Railroad, saved his money, and bought property. A self-made man, in just five years H. B. owned his own home and three other properties: two adjoining houses down the street, which he rented out for extra income, and a general store.

Charlotte is the seat of Mecklenburg County. The Third Ward, where the Kennedys lived, was a mixture of the Old and the New South. Each day H. B. awoke to the sound of roosters crowing at the crack of dawn. He kept hens in his own backyard, ate vegetables from his own garden, and at evening, after a busy day at the store, sat out on the front porch and dozed to the sound of crickets chirping in the fields. But sounds of progress filled the air as well. When the engines of the Magnolia Cotton Mill were running, he could hear them humming all over town.

Art was in Romare Bearden's blood. In spite of all his business activity H. B. found time on weekends to dabble in painting, and his dramatic depiction of Custer's Last Stand hung proudly behind the cash register in the store, side by side with Cattie's portrait of the Great Emancipator, Abraham Lincoln.

Cattie was H. B. and Rosa's only child. She married Richard Bearden, who died young in 1891; their only child was Richard Howard Bearden, called Howard by the family. A source of much pride to his relatives, he grew up lean and darkly handsome and was the family's first college man. (He attended Bennett, in Greensboro, North Carolina.)

His rich childhood memories of Charlotte, North Carolina, and surrounding Mecklenburg County would inform much of Bearden's work, such as School Bell Time, *a 1978 collage from his* Profile/Part I: The Twenties *series.*

Prosperous and aging, H. B. wanted to hold on to the family business. He tried persuading Howard to settle in Charlotte, but his grandson complained that Charlotte was stifling. The economic boom of the late 19th century had gone bust, and work was scarce—especially for young black men. How would he support a family?

H. B. made Howard a proposition. He offered to take him
into the business if he would settle down, but the Jim Crow
laws—anti-Reconstruction legislation enforcing a virtually
all-encompassing segregation of the races—made Howard
bitter. Angry and frustrated, he withstood his grandfather's
threats and pleas and left for the North.

The Train, *a 1974 collage,
hearkens back to Bearden's
childhood memories of the freights
and passenger trains that seemed
always to be departing Charlotte
for some faraway destination.*

In Atlantic City, New Jersey, he met Bessye Johnson Banks, who was fair-skinned, fast-talking, and feisty. Edward Morrow, Romare Bearden's cousin and something of an oral historian in the great griot tradition (in the villages of West Africa, griots were storytellers responsible for orally preserving the history, lineage, and traditions of a people), said that Bessye looked white but was in fact "about 7 parts Italian and 3 parts black." She was a student who had, like Howard, been born in North Carolina and come north in search of a better life.

In 1910 Howard and Bessye were married in Philadelphia, Pennsylvania. Soon, however, they were back in Charlotte. H.B. took the young couple in, and they settled in at the family homestead on South Graham Street. Howard became an organist at the Episcopal church the family attended. (On the side, he was a part-time piano man in local parlors).

Romare (pronounced ro-MARE) was born in "the big house" on South Graham Street. Blond-haired and blue-eyed, he was the family's "fair-haired boy." He was pampered but not spoiled, for Bessye took no nonsense—from him or anybody else. "I could get along with my mother," he recalled. "I didn't need 'the whip.'" But Romare got his way with his aunt Clara, Bessye's sister, who "was much softer."

Surrounded by these three generations of ancestors, Romare enjoyed a happy childhood. His great-grandmother Rosa, who was part Cherokee, took him for long walks along the dirt roads leading to the reservations. There the Cherokees maintained their own schools, their own government, and their own way of life. For the rest of his own life Romare would study and admire other peoples, places, and cultures, as well as his own.

Bearden briefly attended school in Charlotte. He later reminisced about mid-September "books, blackboards, rulers, and fingernail inspections." He remembered his childhood friends from Charlotte, too. There was little Liza, the girl he played with, and there was his cousin Charles "Spinky" Alston. Romie and Spinky spent their summers playing all day on the steps of the Old Mint. Like Romie, Spinky would one day become a noted artist; even as a young child he was fashioning sculptures from the rich red North Carolina clay.

But the memory of Mecklenburg County that Romare Bearden treasured most was of the trains that steamed through Charlotte, journeying north. For endless hours, he would sit and watch them whistle by. "You could tell not only the train," he later recalled, "but also who the engineer was—just by the whistle!"

In the days before jet travel, passenger trains were pure romance. They featured private sleeping compartments, fancy dining cars, and black Pullman porters in crisp white jackets. They carried exotic names like the Sunset Limited. And they were bound for famous cities like New Orleans, Washington, D.C., and New York.

In the mists of memory, Romare Bearden's trains became emblems of exodus. In works like *The Train* and *Train Whistle Blues,* they symbolize great migrations and the transformation of a people in space and time.

For a boy of Bearden's age, Mecklenburg County was idyllic. He would always remember the lady who sold pepper jelly, and the smells of his great-grandfather's garden. He later immortalized them in a series of collages entitled *Memories of Mecklenburg County.* Wherever he might roam, part of him would remain in Charlotte.

But for his parents it was a different story. Once Romare was out shopping with them in the white section of town. Bessye left Howard and little Romie alone for a few minutes while she went into a store. Since she looked white, they knew she could get what she came for without being questioned. Howard walked away for a moment, leaving Romie unattended. When he returned people stared and whispered: what could that "nigger" be doing to that white child? By this time a crowd had gathered. Bessye heard the fracas developing and left the store—just in time.

On another occasion Howard was walking home down South Graham Street. It was pitch-dark. Suddenly, a police detective stopped him and asked where he was from. "New York," Howard said.

Southern policemen were never known for their affection toward "uppity niggers" from the North, so Howard spent the night in jail.

That did it. "My father woke me up around dawn and told me to get my clothes on." Without further ado—and without a word of explanation—Howard packed up his family and left his great-grandfather's house for good. The Beardens were headed north.

3

PITTSBURGH PROFILE

— ♠ —

BETWEEN 1920 AND 1929 Bearden lived on and off in Pittsburgh with his maternal grandmother, Carrie Banks. Together with Charlotte and Harlem, Pittsburgh forms the golden triangle of his life. In those days Pittsburgh was known as the Smoky City. Great steel mills dominated the city's economic life, belching black smoke into the sky continually. The air was so polluted that the morning's clean white shirt was sooty-gray by afternoon.

Grandmother Carrie ran a boardinghouse for steel workers. The house, located on Penn Avenue in the Lawrenceville section of the city, had three floors. The first two had rooms for individual lodgers. The third was a dormitory, where as many as 20 men slept side by side on cots. Each floor had a bathroom down the hall. (On Saturday, "bath day," the lines were especially long.) Everyone ate together in the big dining room downstairs.

In the mornings, Monday through Friday, Romare would watch the trucks rumble off toward the mills, each of them carrying perhaps two dozen workers, recent arrivals from the South. Toiling as many as 12 hours a day, these emigrants earned $40 to $50 a week—fantastic wages at that time. The mills ran 24 hours a day, seven days a week. The conditions inside were hellish, and the men worked stripped to the

After World War I, many blacks from the South traveled north to work in the region's steel mills and factories. Many such emigrants lived in the boardinghouse run by Bearden's maternal grandmother, Carrie Banks.

waist. "When the furnace doors opened, that flame would lick out like a snake's tongue," Bearden recalled to an interviewer years later.

At night the workers straggled back to the boardinghouse, scorched, starving, and exhausted. Grandmother Carrie fed them, rubbed them down with cocoa butter, and sent them to bed. Meanwhile her grandson lay awake at night, listening to the screech of factory whistles in the distance. They reminded him of the trains he had heard whistling through Mecklenburg County. Now he understood: it was those very trains that brought them here.

In the portrait of the artist, the Pittsburgh profile is especially revealing. Pittsburgh is the city where Henry Ossawa Tanner was born. H. O. Tanner (1859–1937), one of the first African-American portraitists, studied under the great Thomas Eakins at the Pennsylvania Academy of Fine Arts. He painted Booker T. Washington and early scenes of African-American domestic life such as *The Banjo Lesson*. Tanner sought to portray humanity in terms of the black experience, as Bearden would later do. For this reason Bearden looked upon Tanner as a kind of founding father of African-American art and later made him one of the subjects of his seminal book *Six Black Masters of American Art*.

A far less likely influence was every bit as deep and lasting, however. One day Romare and his friends were out in Grandmother Carrie's backyard, shooting marbles. A boy in leg braces stood quietly nearby. When he hobbled over to watch them play, they all laughed and called him "crip"—cripple. But the boy would not go away. So they ganged up on him and began to beat him.

When Bearden's grandmother saw what was happening, she intervened. She chased the other boys away, pulled Romare over by the ear, and ordered him to say he was sorry. Romare pouted and hung his

head, scratching doodles in the dust with the tip of his shoe. Reluctantly, he mumbled an apology.

But the crippled kid was cooler than Romare had thought. His name was Eugene, and he kept white doves for pets. Best of all, he could draw. He even gave Romare lessons. Soon Romie and Gene were the best of friends and were spending all their time together.

When Grandmother Carrie was not looking, Gene drew dirty pictures on brown paper bags. One was of a big, dark parlor where a piano player banged out the blues, a cigarette dangling rakishly from his lower lip. Girls in stockings and garter belts lounged on sofas. Some danced with the customers. Meanwhile, a lady called Sadie counted money.

Gene showed the drawing to Romie, who recognized it. Sadie's was a bordello down the street that

Allegheny Morning Sky, a 1978 collage, makes use of Bearden's recollections of his childhood years in Pittsburgh. Note the resemblance of the skyline visible through the window on the left to the photograph at the opening of this chapter.

In 1978, Bearden created this collage, Farewell, Eugene, *based on his recollections of the funeral of his childhood friend Eugene, who had been his first artistic inspiration.*

Romie passed every day on his paper route, sometimes even stopping to sneak a peek inside. But he had never seen anything quite like this. Gene had drawn a kind of cross section: Sadie's from the inside out! Romie was amazed.

Curious about what the boys were up to, Grandmother Carrie soon came in. Romie and Gene tried
desperately to hide the picture, but they were caught
red-handed. Grandmother Carrie was furious. Where
had they seen such things? she demanded to know.

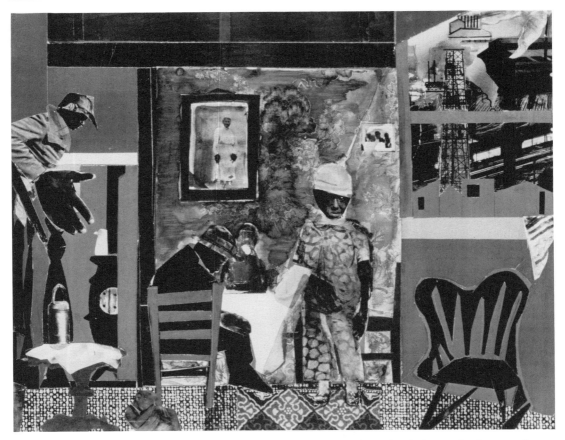

Millhand's Lunch Bucket *is another 1978 Bearden collage that draws on his childhood familiarity with the Southern black emigrants who manned Pittsburgh's steel mills.*

Gene fessed up: he had peeked through the cracks in the floor; he lived at Sadie's; Sadie was his mother. Fearful of the influence of such an environment on him, Carrie Banks took the crippled boy to live with her at the boardinghouse, where his mother would come to visit him every Sunday. He died about a year later, but his influence lives on in some of the techniques Bearden would employ in his collages and photomontages. Indeed, one of the most heartfelt of those works was entitled *Farewell, Eugene* and constituted Bearden's artistic remembrance of his friend's funeral.

Bearden would always remember the steel mills and clapboard houses of Pittsburgh. He would remember, too, the brothels and dark alleyways. He took it all in, remembered it, and portrayed it frankly in such works as *Pittsburgh*, *Pittsburgh Memory*, and *Pittsburgh Recollections*. Pittsburgh remembers Bearden, too; one of his murals is installed in the city's public transportation system.

By 1927 Carrie Banks had left the shanties of Lawrenceville behind and had moved to East Liberty, on the other side of the tracks. It was a better neighborhood, far from the noise, dirt, and danger of the steel mills. There, Bearden completed his last two years of high school.

In the mornings, he walked to Peabody High, where he excelled in math and science. Romare had inherited Bessye's brains, and his mother, hoping he would become a doctor, encouraged these interests. After school, there were sports. Romare also had his father's athletic ability. The coming of autumn, winter, and spring heralded football, basketball, and baseball season, each in its turn, and he marked the passage of the years by the transition from one sport to the next.

On weekends there were the movies, which cost 11 cents. Still interested in art, Bearden entered and won a movie-poster contest. The prize was $25 and a year's free admission to the cinema.

Art and industry are recurrent themes in Romare Bearden's life, but his fascination with industrial work did not mean that he was personally suited for it. In 1927 he got a firsthand taste of the mills. That summer was hotter than usual, but the furnaces were hotter still. "Just opening the door," he recalled, "was like opening the furnace to hell," and after just one stint on the night shift he asked for a new assignment. He was told to paint the roof of the mill, but in the noonday sun the roof was almost as hot as the furnaces, and he requested another transfer. This time he was made to move steel from the mill to a barge on a nearby canal. But Bearden was still a boy, and this was man's work. Once, laboring under too heavy a load, he fell into the canal. Next, he tried his hand at chipping out imperfections in steel with a hydraulic drill, but when he realized that one slip of the high-powered instrument could mean the loss of a toe, it was time to request another reassignment.

Bearden was a good kid, so they gave him one last chance. His assignment was to sort steel—high-grade surgical material to be shipped all over the country. Bearden looked around and sized up the situation: his partner was strong but almost illiterate; he, on the other hand, was bright but not nearly as strong. An idea took shape. He invented an alphabetical sorting system: A for Atlanta, B for Baltimore, C for Chicago, and so on. His partner would be the brawn and he the brains of the operation. Bearden marked. His partner carried. Together, they made a good team. Everyone was happy, and Bearden kept his job.

Bearden graduated from Peabody High in 1929. Soon he would be leaving Pittsburgh. But like his great-grandfather before him, Bearden was enterprising. That last summer, he took another job.

Mr. Druett ran a nightclub in town. He was a shady character, to say the least. An outright racist, Druett supported the local Ku Klux Klan. During Prohibition he was a bootlegger and ran a speakeasy on the lakefront. To top it all off, he was mixed up with the mob.

Druett knew Romare was black—though he did not look it, his grandmother clearly did—but he liked him anyway. On weekdays he let Romare wash his enormous car. He also let him chauffeur his enormous wife, who sat in the backseat eating candy all day.

On the weekends Romare worked at Druett's lakefront speakeasy. As the police took their bribes in booze, there was never too much real danger of trouble. Since young Romare had an air of innocence about him, Druett had him carry the cash in his pants pocket, just in case.

One night while Druett was away a man came in and made reservations for a party of six. He then left, saying that he was going to get the others and would be right back. A party of six came back, all right—with shotguns.

Women screamed or fainted dead away. The robbers lined everybody up against the wall. First they took cash and watches from the men. Next, they took jewelry and fur coats from the women. Finally, one of the gunmen came over to Romare.

"Hands up!" he snarled. Romare was terrified. He just knew he was going to get shot—or worse. The gunman looked him up and down. "Put your hands down, kid," he ordered. Waving the shotgun in the direction of the cash register, he demanded, "How much is in that thing?" Romare swallowed hard, then eased over to the register, praying that no one would notice the bulge in his pants pocket. Pleading that business had been slow, he opened the register. Clearly displeased, the holdup man reached in, took $200 and a few bottles of bootleg whiskey, and made his getaway.

Later, Bearden handed over to Druett the bankroll he had pocketed. The gangster was so grateful that he rewarded Romare with enough money to pay for his first year of college. ◖◗

4

HOME TO HARLEM

W. E. B. Du Bois at work in the offices of Crisis, *the journal of the National Association for the Advancement of Colored People (NAACP), which he edited. One of the foremost American intellectuals of his day, Du Bois was one of the many residents of Harlem who made the community intellectually stimulating for the young Bearden.*

O N LEAVING THE SOUTH the Beardens initially settled in Canada, where Howard became a steward with the Canadian Railroad. For a time, the Beardens lived in the province of Saskatchewan, where black families had been emigrating since the days of the Underground Railroad, the abolitionist escape route. For generations this influx was the core of Canada's black population.

In the 1920s Howard moved his family back to the United States and into Harlem, the mecca of black America. At the time Harlem was a multiethnic enclave, home to large numbers of Italians and Jews as well as blacks. There were shady trees, safe, clean streets, and well-kept parks with ponds and fields where West Indian immigrants played cricket. New York was America's greatest city, and Harlem was America's most conspicuous black community. For Bearden, it constituted a third home. He spent most of his time with his immediate family in New York City, where he received the greater part of his schooling, with occasional long periods in Pittsburgh, including his last two years of high school. Many summers and vacations were spent in Charlotte.

At the time the Beardens arrived in Harlem the community was at the center of an explosion of African-American cultural achievement known as the Harlem Renaissance. Poets and painters, preachers and politicians, dancers and musicians, entrepreneurs and educators, all rubbed elbows with pimps and prostitutes. At one time or another Harlem was home to just about every luminary of African-American culture, including Paul Robeson, Jean Toomer, Josephine Baker, Bessie Smith, Langston Hughes, and Bill "Mr. Bojangles" Robinson. "The confines where you lived were so narrow," Bearden observed, "that you met everybody. W. E. B. Du Bois and James Weldon Johnson lived on 135th Street. Just a little farther up were Claude McKay, Langston Hughes, and Countee Cullen."

The Beardens arrived just in time to experience these heady days, though it took them a little while to get established. At first, with work hard to find, Howard and Bessye rented a series of shabby rooms. Then they moved in with Howard's great-aunt Anna before settling in their own place at 154 West 131st Street, on a block of immaculate brownstones. The apartment overlooked the neighborhood playground. From his bedroom window Romare could see the Lafayette Theater or Connie's Inn, where elegantly dressed entertainers such as Bessie Smith came and went. The sound of music wafted out from the club's doors, which were open to the street. On warm summer evenings, in those days before air-conditioning, neighbors sat out on the stoop to enjoy the evening, the music, and each other.

Although a highly intelligent, educated man, an amateur classicist and grammarian who could tell you off the top of his head the origin, meaning, and function of almost any word in English, Howard Bearden was a "good-timing" intellectual. He continued as always to play the piano on the side and lived only for good times, good music, and good liquor. Though he eventually found steady employment with the New York City Department of Health, the dominant figure in the household was Romare's mother, Bessye.

After stints managing the ticket office of the Lafayette Theater and working in a real estate firm, Bessye became New York bureau chief of the *Chicago Defender*, which was in all likelihood the most influential black newspaper in the country at the time. Tireless and extroverted, with a strong interest in politics, she also became a noted community leader who served on countless committees—"She was on every kind of committee; she'd come home, and then right back out she'd go," her son later recalled—and made her family's apartment a common meeting place for the movers and shakers in Harlem's artistic, political, and social worlds. Brainy, beautiful, and brash—she thought nothing of strolling into Howard's favorite watering hole, announcing her own last call, flinging his pajamas in his face, and hauling him off home—she was also steady, sober, and industrious. Over the years her talents (and her light skin, which allowed her to pass for white) enabled her to hold a variety of important posts, including, from 1935 until her death in 1943, a position as an inspector with the Internal Revenue Service. At various times she was also secretary and later chairwoman of the New York City School Board, a member of the Negro Women's Democratic Club, an executive board member of the Urban League, and a founder of the National Council of Negro Women. Her close friend and colleague in many of these endeavors was the eminent black educator Mary McLeod Bethune.

The spirit of the Harlem Renaissance flourished in Bessye Bearden's parlor on 131st Street, where she presided over brilliant gatherings of blacks from every field. Howard played duets with jazz greats Fats Waller and Duke Ellington, a distant cousin on the Kennedy side; Waller would even buy Bearden's first oil paintings. Paul Robeson regularly stopped by, and

Bessye Bearden was the dominant presence in the Bearden household. A political activist with friends from every walk of life, Bessye was a fixture in Harlem.

the house was always full of relatives, friends, and Siamese cats. "It was like a revolving door," Bearden remembered.

In Harlem, as elsewhere in the United States, the good times came to an end with the stock market crash of October 1929 and the subsequent collapse of the entire American economy known as the Great Depression. With the unemployment rate for the country as a whole approaching 33 percent at some periods of the 1930s, blacks were harder hit by the collapse than any other segment of the American population, but the Beardens were more fortunate than most. Bessye's connections and abilities enabled her to hold on to her jobs and even to send Romare to college. Indeed, her dedication to her only child was legendary. Inevitably, friends said, she would steer conversation to her child with the question, "Now, what can you do for *my* baby?"

Initially Bearden attended Lincoln University, a prestigious black educational institution in Pennsylvania, but after a year he transferred to Boston University (BU). He majored in mathematics, leading his mother to harbor hopes that he would become a doctor, but he had become at least as interested in drawing and art as he was in his classwork.

He also continued to display his outstanding athletic ability. A natural athlete whose skills flourished even without much cultivation, Bearden starred for two years as a pitcher for the BU baseball team, and in the summers he hurled for a semiprofessional team, the Boston Tigers. Professional baseball was still rigidly segregated, of course, but Bearden competed against many of the greatest talents of the Negro leagues, including Satchel Paige, and was apparently good enough to consider a professional career himself. On one memorable occasion he pitched for the BU nine in an exhibition game against the Philadelphia Athletics, who then boasted one of the greatest lineups ever assembled. The only hit he allowed was a home run to future Hall of Famer Al Simmons; so impressive was his performance that Philadelphia's legendary owner and manager Connie Mack offered him a major-league contract if he were willing to try to pass for white. Bearden refused and soon thereafter gave up the game in favor of art, where he had already enjoyed some success in the form of cartoons and drawings published in the Boston University newspaper.

That decision was instrumental in helping Bearden determine another change of course—to return to his family's apartment in Harlem and attend classes at New York University. Though he persisted with mathematics as his course of study, the move was determined mostly by his desire to be near New York City's thriving art scene.

In New York Bearden was exposed to all kinds of new artistic influences, chief among them the works of such modernist giants as Pablo Picasso and the scathing political cartoonist and painter George Grosz. His own cartoons, which were becoming increasingly political, appeared in the New York University *Medley* and—after his graduation with a degree in mathematics in 1935—the Baltimore *Afro-American*, a black newspaper. Though cartoonists and illustrators could count on steady work and earn decent money by the standards of the art world, Bearden had greater artistic ambitions for himself. His commitment to art was by now so total that he rejected all of the obvious ways of earning a living available to someone with a mathematics degree, such as teaching math or becoming an accountant.

His artistic ambition had been inflamed by an exhibition given at the Museum of Modern Art in 1935, the year of his graduation. Entitled *African Negro Art*, it inspired in Bearden the possibility of creating meaningful modern art from his own experience as a black man and from the cultural legacy of his ancestors. He began to think of ways to incorporate African influences into his own art. If Picasso had boldly used African masks in his work, so could he, it seemed. Alain Locke, the scholar responsible for articulating many of the aesthetic

continued on page 57

THE PAINTINGS OF
ROMARE BEARDEN

Three Folk Musicians, 1967

Black Manhattan, 1969

Showtime! 1974

Miss Bertha and Mr. Seth, 1978

Early Carolina Morning, 1978

Slapping Seventh Avenue with the Sole of My Shoe, 1981

Autumn Lamp (Guitar Player), 1983

The Piano Lesson, 1984

Quilting Time, 1985

continued from page 48

principles of the Harlem Renaissance, had written that African art "presents to the Negro artist in the New World a challenge to recapture his lost heritage." Here, then, Bearden was quick to realize, was a historic opportunity for black artists to reveal the beauty and complexity of the black experience "in a vital, new, and radically expressive art."

Though African-American artists often found it difficult to earn a living during the Great Depression, there were many sources of moral and artistic encouragement. Bearden associated himself with two such artistic groups, the Harlem Artists Guild and a more informal, loose association known as 306.

The Harlem Artists Guild, which met at the 135th Street YMCA, had been formed by the sculptor Augusta Savage, Bearden's cousin Charles Alston, and several other black artists for the purpose of gaining more grants and funding for African-American artists from the Federal Arts Project (FAP) of the Works Progress Administration (WPA), a job-creation program begun by President Franklin D. Roosevelt. Established in 1935, the WPA/FAP employed thousands of artists to uplift and beautify the nation with murals, monuments, and other large-scale public works.

The 306 group consisted of artists, writers, and musicians who gathered at 306 West 141st Street, a building that contained workshops, studio space, art supplies, and even living quarters. Charles Alston maintained an apartment in the rear, and famous black writers such as Richard Wright, Langston Hughes, and Countee Cullen regularly dropped by. With few sources of private patronage, black artists were forced to rely on each other for encouragement and sustenance. "In the 30s," Bearden recalled, "everyone would gather together and encourage each other. Countee Cullen would have a party for the artists every month or so and put up a few paintings to sell. You would get only $10, $15 or $25, but it kept up morale." The manager of the Savoy Ballroom did his part by sometimes letting in the artists free so that they could drink and talk while enjoying the swinging sounds of big bands led by Tommy Dorsey, Cab Calloway, Duke Ellington, and Benny Goodman.

Perhaps naturally, starving artists sympathized with the plight of the poor. In response to the bleak social realities of the Great Depression they portrayed life as they saw it: down and dirty. This "social realism" became the dominant movement in art. Along with the Mexican muralist Diego Rivera and the American painter Ben Shahn, George Grosz, whose politically charged work had forced him to flee Adolf Hitler's Nazi Germany, was preeminent among the social realists. Since 1932, Bearden had been dropping in informally at the master's classes at the Art Students League; in 1936 he began formal lessons with Grosz.

It was Grosz who first encouraged Bearden to paint. Impressed by his obvious talent and dedication, he arranged for Bearden to study free at the Art Students League. Always scholarly by temperament, Bearden began looking into past masters of carica-ture: Dürer, Daumier, and especially Pieter Breughel, the great Flemish satirist. "I studied from 7:00 until 10:00 every night, drawing from the model. Every day I was learning something." At the same time, Bearden continued to contribute cartoons to the Baltimore *Afro-American* and to such national magazines as *Life*. His sketches of the time depicting tenements and soup kitchens evidence his ever-growing social and political awareness as well as Grosz's continuing influence.

Although Bearden's art would always be implicit-ly political, it would also stress the personal, and

The corrosive political commentary in the work of the German artist George Grosz, such as this 1928 piece The Agitator *(who looks not unlike Adolf Hitler, whose National Socialist movement was then on the rise), caused it to be suppressed in his homeland and eventually forced his emigration to the United States. Grosz taught Bearden at the Art Students League. From him, Bearden said, he learned how to "really observe."*

friendship would be a recurring motif in both his art and his life. His life would be rich in friendship, and friendship in turn would enrich his art. No friend would be more crucial to his development than the painter Stuart Davis, whom he met in 1938.

Davis was a jazz fanatic. He would sit for hours on end listening to recordings of pianist Earl "Fatha" Hines. He even named his son after him. Bearden visited Davis regularly. They hung around in the Village together, visiting the jazz clubs and talking endlessly about art. Unlike many of Bearden's artist friends, Davis loved baseball. The two men went often to see the Brooklyn Dodgers play at Ebbets Field, where they munched on peanuts and hot dogs and swilled cold beer. From baseball statistics the conversation inevitably turned to the aesthetics of jazz and art, which Davis saw as inextricably linked. "You got to look at things as musical beats," Davis would tell Bearden. From Davis, Bearden learned to see and paint art the way a musician hears and plays music. "Listen to what he isn't playing," Davis would say about his beloved Earl Hines. "What you don't need is just as important as what you do need." Like rests in music, Davis would insist, blank spaces in painting create rhythm. Because of Davis, harmony and rhythm in painting became as important to Bearden as color. Davis forever altered the way Bearden made music on canvas.

But though Bearden was growing artistically, he was unable to make ends meet as a cartoonist, and in 1938 he took a job as a welfare caseworker for the New York City Department of Social Services. Though this represented a setback in terms of the amount of time he could devote to his art, he still managed to paint on weekends and at night. The steady income even allowed him, with the help of his friend and fellow artist Jacob Lawrence, to obtain his first studio, at 33 West 125th Street, though he was forced to give it up once winter came and he realized that it was unheated. His mother came to the rescue, however, and, using her real estate contacts, found him a new place at 243 West 125th Street, right above the Apollo Theater.

There Bearden could paint to the sounds of jazz from the theater below. Claude McKay, author of *Harlem Shadows* and one of the most famous writers of the Harlem Renaissance, was his neighbor. So was Jacob Lawrence. His bird's-eye view of the goings-on below on 125th Street, Harlem's main drag, were a constant source of inspiration. "I do not need to go looking for 'happenings,' " he said of the sometimes fantastic scenes in his early paintings; he needed only to look out his window.

But that comment was made later, in the full blush of a more mature artistic confidence. At first in his new studio Bearden found it difficult to put anything on the brown paper on his easel. One night, after several hours of blank frustration, he decided to go for a walk with Claude McKay. As they descended the stairs they heard keys jingling in the hallway—a well-recognized signal used by Harlem's prostitutes to solicit a customer. But in this case, in the opinion of the writer and the painter, the woman was spectacularly unsuited for her line of work, for she was one of the ugliest women they had ever seen. McKay whispered that she looked like a freight train, and the two young men giggled.

"She said, 'Two dollars, boys,' " Bearden later remembered. "Then she said, 'A dollar?' Then, 'Fifty cents?' Then, 'A quarter?' Finally, she said, 'For God's sake, just take me.' She was pathetic."

The woman's name was Ida. Bearden told her she was in the wrong business, and he asked his mother to find her a job, which she did. Gratefully, Ida came every Saturday to clean Bearden's studio. After several weeks she noticed his easel. Now it was her turn. "Is that the same piece of brown paper from last week and the week before? Aren't you supposed to be an artist? I don't see any painting." Bearden told her he had no ideas. "You told me I was in the wrong profession!" she teased. "Why don't you paint me?"

When he failed to respond, she knew the reason why. "I know what I look like," she admitted. "But when you can look and find what's beautiful in me, then you're going to be able to do something on that paper of yours." What the woman had said struck home. "That always sort of stuck with me, what she said," Bearden remembered years later, and he began to search for his subject matter—and for beauty—in the things and people he knew. "Paint what you know," friends had told him, but it had never really sunk in until the encounter with Ida. "I thought about who I was and what I liked, and I began to paint pictures of the people I knew and remembered down South," Bearden said. It was his first significant artistic breakthrough. The secrets of the canvas were revealed to him. Ida's insight had cured his artistic impotence. He learned, and was therefore able to teach others, to see the beauty in black.

The works that resulted were still heavily influenced by Rivera, Grosz, and Shahn. Done mostly with tempera on paper, they are frank depictions of rural blacks executed in earthy terra-cottas reminiscent of the clay of his native North Carolina. Bearden's first conscious attempts to recapture his own past—works such as *Two Women in a Landscape*, *The Visitation*, and *Folk Musicians*—brought him his first public acclaim. *Fortune* magazine used his *Factory Workers* as a front-cover illustration for an issue entitled "The Negro's War," and in 1940 and 1941 the Downtown Gallery represented Bearden in a major group exhibition, *American Negro Art: 19th and 20th Centuries*. Best of all, in the spring of 1940 Bearden's friend Ad Bates gave him his first solo exhibition at 306, and older artists were beginning to single him out as an artist to watch. Romare Bearden, it seemed, had arrived. ❦

5

WRESTLING WITH
THE ANGELS
❧

An artist at work in the
picturesque Montmartre district of
Paris, France, in the early 1950s.
At this time, Bearden joined
many other black American artists
in the French capital, where
living was cheap and racial
discrimination was rare.

BUT IF THE ART world at large now knew who
Romare Bearden was, he himself was not quite so
sure. As a person and as an artist, Bearden had yet to
find himself, and if no longer empty, his canvas, he
would come to feel, was full of false starts. Art is the
formal representation of life, and the painter, in order
to do his work, must first experience life—and live
to tell the story. From 1942 to 1953 life taught
Bearden some hard lessons. During this time, he later
said, he wrestled with the angels, and his inner
strength was sorely tried.

Not long after the United States' entry into
World War II, Bearden enlisted in the army, which,
like all the armed services at that time, was still
segregated. He was assigned to the 372d Infantry
Division, an all-black regiment with a record of
distinguished combat service. Bearden, however, received only stateside posts during the war, at various
military installations in Alaska, Arizona, Kentucky,
Massachusetts, New Jersey, and even in New York
City, where he guarded the subways against potential
sabotage.

For Bearden personally the greatest casualty of the
war years, aside from his painting—he was able to
visit the studio occasionally while posted in New
Jersey and New York—was his mother. Bessye Banks

Bearden died of the postoperative effects of gall bladder illness on September 16, 1943. Her son had seen her for the last time several weeks earlier; unable to speak, she had bid him farewell by making the "V for victory" sign with her hand. Though the death was hard on him, it was worse for his father, whose drinking accelerated in the aftermath of his wife's passing to the point where it threatened his sanity. He recovered somewhat and lived until 1960, but he was never again the same in mind or spirit.

Bearden was fortunate enough to be able to hold on to his studio during the war years, and in 1944 the celebrated African-American painter William H. Johnson brought Caresse Crosby, owner of the G Place Gallery in Washington, D.C., there to look at Bearden's work. She was sufficiently impressed to offer him his first solo show at a major gallery.

Entitled *The Passion of Christ*, the exhibition took place in June 1945 and consisted of watercolors inspired by Biblical imagery and the works of the artists of the Italian Renaissance, painted by Bearden between 1940 and 1941. A practicing if not zealous Episcopalian, Bearden had a solid religious grounding and knew his Bible. In works such as *Adoration of the Magi*, *The Last Supper*, and *The Resurrection*, thick, dark lines, like the lead that separates sections of stained glass, reveal the influence of medieval church windows. Yet the colors, reds and blues and yellows, are radiant.

Critical opinion on Bearden's work during this period was mixed. One writer dismissed it as "colonial Cubism diffused into WPA-style figure painting," but Barrie Stavis, a longtime friend and early admirer, thought it promising. "The first time I saw one of his watercolors, it bowled me over," he said. "There was never any question in my mind that Romie would emerge as a major artist."

As the criticism of the Washington show indicated, Bearden was still seeking—unsuccessfully, in the eyes of some—to incorporate the elements of European modern art into his own personal vision. As evident now as the early influence of Grosz were the cubist tenets of Pablo Picasso, the Spaniard who had clearly established himself as the dominant artistic figure of the 20th century. Cubism, which Picasso had pioneered in tandem with a French painter, Georges Braque, was a movement that sought to portray figures and objects broken down into essential geometric shapes. The idea was to find a way other than the traditional illusion of depth to portray three-dimensional objects in two dimensions.

From the cubists Bearden derived his characteristic combination of rigorous structure and bold,

Though service in the army during World War II prevented Bearden from painting, he enjoyed some of his first commercial success during the war years. In 1944, his work was given its first one-man show, at the G Place Gallery in Washington, D.C., where Bearden (right) discussed his painting Cotton Workers *with his cousin Charles Alston.*

brilliant color, but he was never a slavish adherent of cubist tenets. In later years he would even contend that Picasso and his fellow cubists had misunderstood space—that they had overcrowded their paintings. But in the early 1940s, as Bearden was growing increasingly dissatisfied with social realism, cubism seemed as if it might provide some of the answers to the artistic questions with which he was grappling.

Though by 1945 Bearden was considered—along with Hale Woodruff, William H. Johnson, Charles Alston, and Jacob Lawrence—one of the leading figures among the emerging generation of black artists in America, he was dissatisfied with his work. Deeply concerned with the role of black art and black artists in American society, Bearden believed strongly that art must be an instrument of new vision, not old stereotypes. The African-American artist, he was convinced, could not simply pick up where the ancient African sculptors had left off. The rift had been too wide, and the centuries too long. He saw most contemporary black artists as lacking in orig-inality and looked in vain for a visual equivalent to the depth and complexity he found in giants of modern jazz such as Charlie Parker, Max Roach, Dizzy Gillespie, and Thelonious Monk, who in the early postwar years were reworking and reinventing the traditional forms of the music. Like them, he wanted to portray not just the caricature but the souls of black folk.

His frank depictions of rural black life had an-gered some critics, who accused him of catering to white stereotypes of black people. Bearden acknowl-edged the criticism without necessarily accepting its validity. "I am a man concerned with truth," he fumed, "not flattery," and he insisted on his right to present his artistic truths as he found them. "I will," he said, "continue to paint what I want—and since

I've started down this lonely road, I'd just as well keep going."

In 1945 Bearden took up a new challenge. He began to work with oils. Previously, he had painted almost exclusively in tempera or watercolor. Now he felt that oil on canvas, the medium most often associated with the old masters, would allow him to make the big statement he was striving for.

At first he could not quite get the hang of the new techniques required. Oil dries very slowly, watercolor quite quickly. He would draw a preliminary, or "cartoon," sketch but sometimes find himself unable to successfully execute the final oil. Soon, however, he grew more comfortable with the new medium and made oil additions to the *Passion of Christ* series, which was received very favorably at the fashionable Kootz Gallery in New York City in October 1945. A month later Bearden was featured in a group exhibition at the prestigious Whitney Museum of American Art. At year's end *He Is Arisen*, one of his works from the *Passion of Christ* series, was enshrined in the permanent collection of the Museum of Modern Art, the preeminent institution for 20th-century art—an exceedingly rare honor for a living artist.

That same year, a new friendship was to nourish and enrich Bearden's art. Carl Holty was a German artist who had studied in Munich. As had George Grosz, he had come to New York to escape Hitler's totalitarian regime, but in Europe he had personally known Piet Mondrian, Joan Miró, and many other modernist artists Bearden had admired from afar.

Holty was an abstract painter. In abstract art, the realistic portrayal of life found in figurative art is more or less abandoned in favor of shapes, colors, and patterns. Also called "nonobjective" or "nonrepresentational" art, it dates, like so many developments in 20th-century art, from Picasso and Braque.

By the late 1940s, Bearden was questioning virtually all of his artistic assumptions and had engaged in a renewed study of his artistic forebears, such as Pablo Picasso, whose Woman Weeping *is shown here.*

Bearden quickly grew to trust and admire the older, more experienced Holty and came to regard him as both confidant and mentor. The two artists shared ideas about composition and color as well as their hopes, dreams, and observations on the difficult life of the artist in society. From Holty, Bearden learned to let feeling and intuition, as much as structure and logic, guide him.

In 1946 Bearden executed a new series of oils entitled *Lament for a Bullfighter*. The paintings recalled the bright colors and swooping lines of the *Passion of Christ* series and were inspired by Picasso and the verses of the Spanish poet Federico García Lorca, whom Bearden had been introduced to in the 1930s by the Harlem Renaissance poet Langston Hughes.

To support themselves, Bearden and Holty had become employees of Samuel Kootz. In exchange for a guaranteed monthly salary they produced a specified amount of work, which Kootz then sold in his gallery for whatever it would fetch. Bearden was unhappy with the arrangement, however—the only one who seemed to be growing richer was Kootz—so in the late 1940s he returned to his job as a social services caseworker. Not until 1968 would he be able to earn a living by his brush alone.

By the end of the decade his prospects as an artist had grown even more grim. In 1948 the Kootz Gallery closed, and Bearden found himself without a dealer. Abstract expressionism, which wedded emotionally charged color to nonobjective or nonrepresentational form, was the new rage; Bearden's style of art, figurative and cubist-influenced, was suddenly and distinctly out of fashion.

Though Bearden had genuine respect for the artistic achievement of the abstract expressionists, particularly the members of the so-called New York school—Robert Motherwell, Franz Kline, Mark Rothko, Jackson Pollock, and Willem de Kooning— he was disgusted by the fickleness and machinations he found on the business side of the art world. Bold, forceful, and even strident, the work of the abstract expressionists, Bearden said admiringly, represented a distinctively "American way of seeing." These new painters, he believed, had successfully come to terms with one of the most positive elements in American culture—its music.

But the art marketplace, Bearden felt, was different—greedy, stupid, and rigged. Few dealers, patrons, or critics actually knew good art from bad, and those who did promoted only what was fashionable and would sell. He had learned the hard way that there was more to fame and fortune than just talent. A painter must be more than just an artist; he must be a salesman, politician, and diplomat as well. "There is a lot more to it than just putting . . . paint on canvas," he later explained.

Bearden knew he was talented. He even knew, deep down, that given time he might one day be great. He knew what he wanted to say, but he was just not sure how to say it.

He was not yet totally discouraged, however. More deeply than ever, he began to study spatial relationships in painting, poring over books on Byzantine mosaics and early Italian Renaissance painting. For Bearden, who had always seen something scientific in art theory, the studio became a laboratory. "To find the answers to problems [of form and color] is all that really interests me," he confided to Holty.

Always encouraging, Bearden's mentor was nonetheless certain that he would not find what he needed in the United States. "I want you to go to Paris," he wrote Bearden. (Discouraged himself, Holty had left New York not long after the Kootz Gallery closed.) "Your painting is wonderful, but you need something new." The idea appealed to Bearden, who agreed that he needed a different perspective and was eager to study the European branch of his artistic heritage at its source.

For artists, Paris had always been the most important city in the world, and in the 1950s, it still had its attractions. Picasso and Henri Matisse, the French painter whose influence on the art world had been almost as great as Picasso's, were still in residence. For black American artists, in particular, Paris had always exerted an especially strong pull; the French had been among the first to recognize the genius of many black jazz artists, and American blacks welcomed the freedom from discrimination they experienced there. In the years immediately following World War II, the city was particularly attractive to

American GIs because the ruined French economy resulted in low prices that allowed veterans to live relatively comfortably there on the $75 monthly stipend they received under the GI Bill.

With his stipend, Bearden took a room in a little boardinghouse at 5, rue de Feuillantines. The monthly $40 rent left him plenty to spend in the cafés where he seemed to spend most of his time, talking art and politics with fellow American expatriates. Though he took classes in philosophy at the Sorbonne, Paris's ancient and renowned university, and read deeply from the works of André Gide and other contemporary French writers and thinkers—pursuits that according to his cousin Edward Morrow "gave him the edge" in his art—most of his time and energy was devoted to simply experiencing all that Paris had to offer. He befriended James Baldwin, the young and promising expatriate African-American writer, and read from his work in progress, a first novel that would be published as *Go Tell It on the Mountain*. He dined as the guest of Constantin Brancusi, one of the world's foremost sculptors, who boasted also of being "one of the world's two or three greatest cooks." He met Picasso, who was by this time, in Bearden's words, as much a tourist attraction as "going to see the Eiffel Tower." He visited more traditional tourist sights, such as the Cathedral of Notre Dame, which to him "seemed the most immense structure on earth." While seated outside at a crowded café one day, he watched in amazement as his fellow patrons rose as one and gave a standing ovation to a frail old man who was passing slowly by, supported by a younger man and woman. The old man was Matisse; Bearden thought it marvelous that in Paris an artist could receive the kind of adulation Americans reserved for movie stars. The crowd was applauding a man who, through his art, helped others to see life in a new light. The master, in turn, came over and

Bearden's unending quest for new means of artistic expression took him back to the frescoes of the early Italian Renaissance. He did not believe that as an African American his art had to be confined to political or social issues. "There is only one art and it belongs to all mankind," he said. "Examine the forms of any culture and one becomes aware of the patterns that link it to other cultures and peoples."

shook hands with everyone. "Matisse was delighted," Bearden reported.

Despite such magical moments, Bearden did not remain long in love with Paris—"the place of dreams," he called it early on in his stay. His inability to speak the language wore on him, and he found the Parisians "standoffish." He had difficulty managing his free time—too much freedom, he said, was worse than none—and often found it easier to spend the day in conversation or daydreaming at a café than at the hard work of painting. Most important, he came to believe that Paris's heyday as the world art capital was drawing to close. "Art goes where energy is," he said, "and Paris is tired." The abstract expressionists had made New York the new capital, and in the summer of 1951, after just about a year in France, he returned there.

But once in New York, Bearden could only think of how to get back to Paris. He applied for a Fulbright

Fellowship, but his application was denied. Through his open window above the Apollo Theater, he listened to the sound of the blues in the night and tried to paint, but now the music was more of a distraction than an inspiration. He produced little and sold less.

Desperate and depressed, he devised what he later called a "wildcat scheme to get rich quick." Composer friends had taught him to write song lyrics, and he decided to devote his attention to songwriting with the intention of composing just one hit number that would leave him rich enough to devote all his time to painting. But the means to an end became a means of escape: over the next several years—a span in which he wrote about a dozen songs, one of which was even recorded by the extremely popular Billy Eckstine—he simply, in his own words, "turned away from painting." Finally, friends convinced him that he was wasting his talent.

Deeply unhappy, he began to suffer troublesome physical symptoms. Abdominal pains left him convinced he was riddled with cancer, while frequent shooting pains in his chest scared him into believing he was suffering heart trouble. Doctors found nothing, but one day in 1953 he simply collapsed while walking down the street. He woke up in Bellevue Hospital—in the psychiatric ward. "You blew a fuse," the doctor told him. Exhaustion, stress, poor diet, and a lack of sleep had pushed him over the edge into a nervous breakdown.

To Bearden, it felt like the end. His mother had died, his once promising career had careened off track, and now this. His world was ruined, and he felt he could not continue. Bearden called his father to tell him he was dying. ❦

6

THE PREVALENCE
OF RITUAL

Bearden and his wife, Nanette Rohan, at an exhibition of the artist's work. Friends credit Nanette with providing Bearden with the inner peace that enabled him to resume painting.

BEARDEN BELIEVED IT was the end. In fact, it was a new beginning. His life and art were both about to be revitalized, and the next 35 years would be among his happiest and most productive.

If behind every great man there is a great woman, behind Romare Bearden there were several. First there was his mother Bessye. Then there was his grandmother Carrie. Now there was another; his recovery was aided by a woman named Nanette Rohan. She was a dancer, pretty and petite, whose parents had come to America from the island of St. Martin, in the Caribbean. She liked to say that she, too, had been born on an island: Staten Island, in New York City.

Appropriately enough, Romare and Nanette met at a benefit for the victims of a West Indies hurricane. His own life had been a whirlwind, but Nanette would prove to be the calm at the eye of the storm. Bearden's friends gave her much of the credit for his being able to resume his creative life. "She picked up the pieces and put them back together," his cousin, Edward Morrow, said. "Now that was collage!"

In 1954, in September—the month of his birth and of his mother's death—Romare and Nanette Bearden were wed. Not until his death 35 years later did they part. Bearden showed Nanette Europe. They toured Italy—Genoa, Venice, Florence—Switzerland, and, of course, Paris. In spring, they strolled the narrow, winding streets and visited the galleries. And Nanette showed him the Caribbean. Its sand and sea and sky would color all his later work. Its light and warmth and color would seduce them both into coming back, year after year. Eventually the Caribbean became their second home.

In New York, the Beardens set up house at 357 Canal Street in Soho, where Little Italy meets Chinatown. At one point they occupied two floors of the building; their living quarters were on the fifth, Romare's studio space on the second.

Bearden had second thoughts about resuming his art career. But Nanette believed in him. Encouraged by her belief, he began to paint again. With this support, starting over again was easier. But it was not easy, for his technique had grown rusty.

His aesthetic education, however, was broad and deep. If travel broadens the mind and reading is traveling into the mind's interior, then Bearden was a world-class traveler. Literature, philosophy, and art history were just a few of his points of interest.

In the journals of Eugène Delacroix, Bearden read how the great French artist had copied the old masters. Delacroix went religiously to the Louvre, taking along his paints and easel. Painstakingly, stroke by stroke, he attempted to duplicate the masters' effects. This example inspired Bearden. Delacroix, one of the greatest painters in history, had humbled himself to learn the secrets of art at the feet of the great. Bearden decided to try this himself.

He began at the beginning. The early Italian Renaissance—Giotto and Duccio—was first. Next came the late Renaissance: Veronese, Rembrandt, and Vermeer. He ended with Manet, Monet, and Matisse, the modern heirs of Delacroix. For two years, Bearden did little but copy these and other masters.

It was the perfect restorative. He learned a great deal, for example, about shapes and scale. He felt he had always had a good eye for color and composition, but he had encountered trouble "scaling up" his work, enlarging it effectively from a smaller model. From the old masters, Bearden learned the rules. But he also learned something even more important: how to break them.

Far from cramping Bearden's style, these exercises liberated it. For him, masterpieces were not rigid, paint-by-the-numbers formulas. They were standards he set for himself to achieve—or if possible surpass. "I think the artist has to be something like a whale," he said, "swimming with his mouth wide open, absorbing everything, until he has what he really needs. When he finds that, he can start to make limitations. And then he really begins to grow."

At this time another mentor came into Bearden's life. Browsing the shops in Soho one Saturday, he met a Chinese bookseller named Wu. Wu was not an artist but a student of art. With Wu, Bearden studied classical Chinese landscape painting.

Bearden was beginning to understand color, but to his eye these paintings seemed flat and washed-out at first. He learned that the great Chinese landscape painters worked in a tradition dating back a thousand years. The Chinese had a different approach to perspective, or depth in painting. Since the Renaissance, Western painters had rendered the illusion of depth in terms of a single vanishing point. Objects seemed to decrease in size as they receded into the picture plane, like a ship on the horizon as viewed from the shore.

But the Chinese painted mountains in the mist as if seen from above, from below, and at eye level, all at the same time. Bearden realized that, by different means but to the same end as the cubist painters, the Chinese landscape painters were depict-

Bearden's study of the artistic masters of the past encompassed the classic Chinese landscape painters, who taught him that there was more than one way to achieve the cubist goal of "simultaneous perspective."

Friends of a man wounded by a policeman call for help during the civil disturbances that occurred in San Francisco in 1966. The mid 1960s were a period of massive social unrest in the African American neighborhoods of many American cities, but Bearden steadfastly resisted the notion that social issues or prescribe political art had to specifically address solutions.

ing the world in terms of a kind of "simultaneous perspective." Bearden began to incorporate this lesson into his own painting. The results would be revolutionary.

At last Bearden felt ready to resume his career, to bare his soul before the public. The prestigious Barone Gallery gave him a solo exhibition, his first since 1949. It reestablished his career, and the critics hailed his return. Bearden was back.

In the 1940s Bearden's style had been a mixture of cubism and WPA social realism. In the late 1950s he turned away from the portrayal of figures altogether. Like the abstract expressionists, he laid his canvases flat on the floor, unstretched and unprimed. He dripped and splattered paint on them. Sometimes he lifted them by the edges, allowing the paint to run freely over the surface. All the while, he listened to jazz in the background. Once he turned the radio on by chance. The music of his friend, the great drummer Max Roach, was playing. Bearden was inspired by the rhythms he heard. "I just took a brush," he recalled, "and painted the sounds."

Color became increasingly important to Bearden. Stuart Davis had told him that "color has a position and a place"; that color creates space. Bearden now saw color in a whole new light, as a language all its own. He began experimenting with oils and acrylic, using them thinned out as if they were watercolors. He learned how to compose in color. "I began to put color down in big marks," he said. He painted in rectangular blocks of color all over the canvas. As in music, Bearden was attempting to paint not just things but the relationships between things.

During the next five years these abstract compositions increased in size and scope. His pictures were tone poems of pure mood and color. Together he and Nanette thought up fanciful titles for them: *Mountains of the Moon* or *A Walk in Paradise Gardens*. This period was a kind of second courtship in Bearden's lifelong love affair with art.

Some critics found these works "pastelly" and "derivative" in comparison with the works of such contemporary masters as Robert Motherwell, Jackson Pollock, or Clyfford Still. Others thought them delicately beautiful. As far as Bearden was concerned, he was growing and evolving. To him, the progression from social realism to copying old masters to abstract expressionism seemed only natural. When he turned his copies of Vermeer paintings upside down, he saw "real, great abstraction." If some abstract expressionist canvases were hard bop, Bearden's were cool jazz.

Bearden's art is deeply concerned with the prevalence of ritual, the ties of birth, baptism, marriage, death, and mourning that bind individuals in so-

When Bearden's massive six-panel collage The Block *was shown as part of the Museum of Modern Art's retrospective show of his work in 1971, its display was accompanied by a tape recording of street sounds and church music.*

ciety. In the early 1960s his art would return to these roots.

Once again, art imitated life. New York's Department of Social Services had reassigned Bearden in 1952. For the next 14 years he worked as a caseworker among the city's Gypsies. Nomads of the city, the Gypsies were dark-skinned Caucasians thought to have originated in India. They later migrated through Persia to Europe and America. A clannish and closed community, they had their own king and presided over their own weddings, births, and burials. For generations the Gypsies had kept their language and customs intact.

The work was not too taxing and left Bearden energy enough to paint at night and on weekends. Besides, the Gypsies afforded him ample opportunity to observe up close that humanity in which his art so richly abounds.

One day, Bearden went over to a Gypsy couple's apartment. The husband was sitting out on the stoop. Suddenly his wife came running down the steps, screaming that their ceiling had caved in.

Bearden and the husband rushed up to find the ceiling collapsed. The wife was unhurt. However, Bearden recalled, the husband "had a club. He quickly hit her on the head, and made a knot! Then, he went down and called the police. He told them that the ceiling had fallen and injured his wife. They got about a year's free rent."

The Gypsies' way of life was fast disappearing in the brutally fast-paced environment of the high, hard city. They were struggling to preserve their culture. In some ways their plight reminded Bearden of the Cherokee Indians back in Mecklenburg County. He saw a parallel with his own people as well. "A lot of the life I knew in certain rural Negro surroundings was passing," he said. He decided to "set down some of my impressions of that life."

He abandoned abstraction in favor of the medium for which he is most famous: collage. This period represents Romare Bearden's artistic homecoming, the flower returning to its roots. "People," he said, "started coming into my work, like opening a door."

The Street *was one of Bearden's highly acclaimed* Projections, *as he called his series of photomontages.*

The 1960s was a revolutionary era. The world, the nation, and the people underwent immense and turbulent changes. The civil rights movement was in full swing, effecting positive change. But it was also the time of the assassins. The killing of President John F. Kennedy in 1963 grieved the entire globe. Malcolm X was murdered in 1965. And in 1968, Bobby Kennedy and Martin Luther King, Jr., were martyred. Abroad, the war raging in Vietnam claimed the lives of thousands of young men. At home angry ghettos in many cities went up in flames, and soldiers patrolled the streets.

In 1963 a group of black artists, composers, writers, and sculptors—Bearden, Hale Woodruff, Charles Alston, and two dozen others—formed the Spiral Group. For three years, on and off, they met to seek broader recognition for black art and to set an aesthetic agenda in keeping with the times. Many of these artists had seen firsthand how disastrous for the Harlem Renaissance the patronizing "darky" vogue of the 1920s had been. They wanted to ensure a different outcome in the 1960s.

It was during the Spiral Group discussions that Bearden first sensed the truly powerful potential of collage. He had always felt the European heritage to be as important to his art as the African American. But he had wondered how to wed the fluidity of street life to classic form and composition, how to bridge the gap between the ghetto and the old masters—between New York's Harlem and Holland's Haarlem. And now he had it.

One of Bearden's earliest collages, *The Circus*, dates from 1961. In 1964, *Projections*, a series of stunning photomontages, marked his return to the reality of the black experience. Images clipped from magazines and newspapers were pasted up and photographically enlarged so that the seams would not show. In the 1940s and 1950s Bearden's work had been distinctive for its vibrant color. Now it was marked by epic scale. The works in the *Projections* series were originally 14 by 18 inches. Bearden blew them up to as much as six by eight feet. The effect was monumental. The striking variations of scale— large hands on small bodies, huge eyes on small heads—made the images seem to recede and leap out from the picture frame simultaneously, conveying a sense of movement.

The effect, as one writer noted, was to re-create the "sights, sounds, debris, and movement that attack the senses as one travels down the streets of a large city." The African mask–like faces are classically formal, yet reveal real depth of feeling. They evoke pity without sentimentality and rage without rant. Given the abstract expressionist work that had gone before, the contrast was all the more startling. The *Projections* were social realism of a radically different kind.

The *Projections* were a triumph. Cordier & Ekstrom gave Bearden's new work a historic exhibition in 1964. In 1965 the *Projections* traveled to the prestigious Corcoran Gallery in Washington, D.C., Bearden's first solo exhibition in a major museum. Critic Dore Ashton called them "a piercing, activist bill of particulars" detailing the "intolerable facts" of the black condition. Robert Hughes called them a "sharply observant, full-blooded, encyclopedic imagery of black life." And the *New York Times* called them "propagandist in the best sense."

But Bearden's intent was to create art, not propaganda. As an African American he was active in the struggle for social justice, but as an artist he was a detached observer. Collage was a way to achieve an expression both more personal and more universal. In collage, from the various elements of the black experience he could create a self-contained world that would not exclude the world at large. It was precisely Bearden's balance of racial sensitivity and aesthetic detachment that made the works so powerful. Thus, the impact of these images has long outlasted mere shock value.

By far the greatest praise came from another artist. Ralph Ellison, author of the famous novel *Invisible Man*, had himself represented the black experience with classic artistry. He wrote of Bearden's *Projec-*

tions, "His meaning is identical with his method. His combination of techniques is in itself eloquent of the sharp breaks, leaps in consciousness, distortions, paradoxes, reversals, telescoping of time and surreal blending of styles, values, hopes and dreams which characterize much of Negro American history."

The *Projections* initiated several series of collages based on Bearden's memories of Mecklenburg County, Pittsburgh, and Harlem, as well as his love of jazz, blues, and the classics. From this point on, Bearden would be known primarily as a collagist. ❧

7

MYSTERIES

❧

FOR 30 YEARS Romare Bearden led a double life. Five days a week, from morning to evening, he worked for money. He devoted as many nights and weekends to art. Art is long, and life is short.

In 1966 things began to change. For the first time Bearden sold enough work to enable him to work at the New York City Department of Social Services only part-time. Two years later, at long last, sales of his work, together with his pension, enabled him to retire fully from the Department of Social Services. That same tragic year—the year of the assassinations of Martin Luther King, Jr., and Robert Kennedy and of fierce rioting in many of the country's inner cities—he had the bittersweet pleasure of seeing one of his works grace the cover of an issue of *Time* magazine devoted to the crisis, and he received a grant from the National Institute of Arts and Letters. Bearden now devoted himself entirely to his art, and for the remainder of the 1960s he produced grand-scale collages on southern themes.

In 1967 an artist friend, Jack Schindler, gave Bearden the use of his Long Island City studio. Just minutes across the river from Manhattan by subway, this quiet, blue-collar neighborhood became work-aday headquarters for the artist in faded overalls. Now, five—sometimes six—days a week, Bearden

A street corner in Watts, a black area of Los Angeles, burns during the rioting that took place there in August 1965.

made the ritual commute from Canal Street, arriving by 10:30 A.M. Rarely varying, this routine became the working rhythm of his life.

Carl Holty had not entirely disappeared from Bearden's life. The two painters were never far from each other's thoughts; for 20 years they had faithfully remained in correspondence. In 1969 this exchange of ideas and insights into painting resulted in a book entitled *The Painter's Mind: A Study of Structure and Space in European Painting.* The painter Hale Woodruff, Bearden's friend and Spiral Group cofounder, called it "required reading." Eventually, Holty returned to New York to teach at Brooklyn College, where he remained until his death in 1973.

Romare and Nanette never had any children. "We had cats," she said. But Bearden had many protegés. He never forgot the generous encouragement he himself received from established artists when he was coming up. In turn, Bearden generously encouraged younger artists—talked to them, taught them, recommended them to people who could further their careers.

Art historian, teacher, student, and curator as well as artist, Romare Bearden was both a founding father and empire builder of black art and arts institutions. With Ernest Crichlow and Norman Lewis he founded the Cinque Gallery in 1969. Funded by a Ford Foundation grant and originally established in New York's Public Theater, Cinque is a nonprofit organization providing young black artists and scholars an outlet for their talents. Some of the first black curators at major New York institutions had been Bearden's protegés at Cinque.

By the 1970s Bearden's fame had spread. He was nationally and internationally renowned. Commissions came his way, and his work was steadily purchased by major museums and collectors. Now he was the master. Younger artists began to seek him out, just as he himself had once sought out George Grosz.

The Block, perhaps the most famous of Bearden's collages, appeared in 1970. Four feet high and 18 feet long, Bearden's *Block* consists of six consecutive panels. Like a filmstrip, it unrolls before the eyes of viewers as they stroll past. Like Eugene's depiction of Pittsburgh's Sadie's, *The Block* contains the whole of a typical street in cross section—Harlem from the inside out. Some installations featured tape-recorded street sounds as well. The total effect is that of piano keys, scaling Harlem's "human comedy" in jazzy themes and variations.

Perhaps the greatest honor of Bearden's career came in 1971. The Museum of Modern Art in New York City had first purchased one of his works for its permanent collection in 1945, a great honor for a living artist, but greater still was the solo exhibition it gave him in 1971. Previously, Bearden had been baptized. Now he was confirmed.

Canonization came in 1972, when Bearden was elected to the National Institute of Arts and Letters. Critics called him the "Breughel of Black Manhattan," not so much one of black America's master artists as a master of American art who happened to be black.

Bearden received a prestigious Guggenheim Fellowship to write a book on African-American art history in 1970. The result was *Six Black Masters of American Art*, a young adult book published in collaboration with Harry Henderson in 1972.

Bearden first visited the Caribbean with Nanette in 1960. New York winters are damp, cold, and gray. And Bearden suffered from the cold: his back stiffened, and his joints ached. The light and warmth and color of the Caribbean revived him. He drank in the colors of the water, the sapphire blue and milky green that varied according to the time of day and position of the sun. He was awestruck by the terrible beauty of the tropical storms, the thunder and lightning that sent his cats scurrying for cover. At once he fell under the spell of the Caribbean's magic and mystery.

He loved it so much that he and Nanette built a house on St. Martin. Nanette still had relatives on the island, and for a time her mother stayed with them. The site they selected for their retreat was off a curving, narrow road on a steep hill overlooking the islands of the bay. Each February and March, as well as in August, they returned. It became their winter and summer retreat.

Year after year, Bearden watched his house rise, watched the stone carvers chisel away at the rocks like master sculptors. Romare was amazed to see huge boulders crumble into tiny pieces at the slightest tap. He asked one of the masons the secret. The man looked up and shrugged his shoulders. One had only to tap the rock delicately, he said, and "listen for its truth." When this "vein of truth was revealed, only a few firm taps were needed." Bearden liked that idea. After all, what was art but an eternal search for the "vein of truth"?

"The house is finished, and looks quite handsome," Bearden proudly wrote to Arne Ekstrom in 1973. It had a commanding view "across the open sea, with the breakers plunging." Steep steps led up to his separate studio, where he left his watercolors in the sun to dry.

In this sea of tranquillity, Bearden was at peace. And this calm in his life and world was, once again, reflected in his art. After the Museum of Modern Art retrospective Bearden abandoned the fragmentary photomontages of the early 1960s. Instead, in his

The gentle skies and translucent sea of the Caribbean world Bearden came to know as a part-time resident of the island of St. Martin inspired a new artistic project, The Odysseus *collages, of which this work,* The Sea Nymph, *is an example.*

later collages, which he called paintings, he used prepainted paper cuttings. The earlier images were characterized by their complexity. The new painting was simplicity itself.

Bearden wanted his work to have "more sonority, more amplitude," and more immediate emotional effect. He cast his palette in the purer, deeper colors of the Caribbean, in the cobalts and indigos of so-called "Bearden blue." The collages of the 1970s are lyrical. And no series Bearden created is more serenely beautiful than his *Odysseus* collages.

Homer's *Odyssey* tells of the wanderings of Odysseus and his crew in the aftermath of the Trojan War. For 10 years he suffers shipwreck and temptation before returning home to his faithful wife, Penelope. In the *Odyssey*, an epic of symbolic departures and returns, Bearden found an ancient echo of his own wandering.

The *Odysseus* series was exhibited at Cordier & Ekstrom in 1977. In 1949 Bearden had made a series of watercolors illustrating Homer's *Iliad*. These were executed in the same style of stained-glass cubism as the *Lament for a Bullfighter* series. On the surface, the *Odysseus* collages seemed just another illustration of classic literature. But Bearden was following in giant steps. He had been deeply influenced by Matisse's classic *Jazz* collages, with their beautiful shapes and bright colors.

In Bearden's hands, the *Odysseus* works become much more than just secondhand classical illustration. Through centuries of conquest and migration, the Mediterranean had been a multiracial, multiethnic civilization of African, European, and Semitic peoples, much like ours today. Boldly, brilliantly, Bearden reimagined the voyage over Homer's "wine-dark sea." His Odysseus is a king, too: "black, but comely," like Solomon in the Bible. His figures are not Greeks in blackface; they are men and women reinvested with the timeless dignity and classical simplicity of the ancients. Stark and noble, they possess the repose of ancient Greek black-figure pottery. In such beautiful collages as *Poseidon*, *The Sea Nymph*, *Home to Ithaca*, and *The Cattle of the Sun*, Bearden successfully *transforms* the *Odyssey* into an African-classical synthesis in blacks and Caribbean blues.

Bearden's firm belief that the ancient myths are very much alive coincided with his belief in the community of spirits through ritual, magic, and the arts. One such source of magic is the Caribbean religion of Obeah. The Obeah claim they can control the sun and moon. There are many impostors, but very few authentic Obeah—and only one high priest. They are conjure artists of the Caribbean.

The mathematician in Romare Bearden admired clarity and logic, but he had his superstitious side as well. Once, as a child in Charlotte, he was playing with some baby chicks in his great-grandfather's backyard. The angry mother hen flew overhead, squawking and flapping her wings. Ever since, he had been terrified of any chicken that was not cooked.

He avoided the number 13 like the plague. While hanging an exhibition once, he realized that it contained just 13 works. He was horrified, shouting, "We've got to put one more in!"

And he hated snakes. Bearden once visited an Obeah conjure woman. He was sitting in her parlor, talking. Suddenly, a "basket opened, and here came this big snake, crawling across her!" He was petrified. In French she asked him mysteriously, "You know what fear is?" His eyes wide, he blurted, "Yes; it's that goddamn snake!"

It was the rare outsider who was allowed to witness Obeah rituals. Drawing on his experiences, Bearden attempted to convey their color and atmosphere in his Obeah series.

But life's ultimate mystery is death. Throughout his life, Romare Bearden witnessed his share of it. "We begin to die," he said, "as soon as we are born." One night, around 2:00 A.M., a friend telephoned. Crying, she said she was calling to tell him that a mutual friend was dead. She begged him not to tell Nanette too soon. It would only upset her. Bearden promised. Then, out of curiosity, he asked what time the friend had died. The woman told him that it had been around 10:00.

Wrapping It Up at the Lafayette, *a 1974 Bearden work, captures the vibrant feel of the Harlem he knew in the 1930s.*

It was now 3:00 A.M. But when Bearden went down to the kitchen, he saw that the clock had stopped at 10:15. He reset it, went back to bed, and thought nothing more about it. Two weeks later, the Beardens attended the funeral. When they returned, Romare noticed something strange. The kitchen clock had stopped again. The time read 10:15. ❧

8

PRELUDE TO FAREWELL

❧

Romare Bearden never published a formal autobiography. Instead, he devoted the last years of his life to a major autobiographical series of collages. Entitled *Profile*, it was inspired by a *New Yorker* profile on him in 1977. Summing up the achievement of Romare Bearden's art, one critic said, "One of the most moving aspects of his work is the way he thought constantly about his heritage." His final years were one long look backward, a prelude to farewell.

From 1978 to 1979, Bearden produced such collage series as Memories of Mecklenburg County. In it and in individual collages like *Maudell Sleet*, he set out to re-create the Charlotte of his childhood. "I never left Charlotte," he always said, "except physically."

In 1980 the *Jazz* series appeared. At once an homage to and variations on a theme of Matisse, it alludes to the various traditional jazz genres and the places where they began: New Orleans, Chicago, Kansas City, and New York. Also in 1980, Charlotte's Mint Museum announced plans for a Romare Bearden retrospective. Charlotte had remembered, recognized, and was now welcoming home her native son.

Bearden pauses while working in his studio during the early 1980s. Though he was now recognized as one of the greatest living American artists, Bearden kept on striving to break new ground in his work.

In Bearden's later years, recollections of his childhood days in Mecklenburg County increasingly served as an inspiration for his work, as in Heat Lightning Eastward, this 1983 piece.

"In my beginning is my end," the poet T. S. Eliot had written in the *Four Quartets*. For Bearden, a lover of poetry—it was "a kind of talking about life," he said—the line had special meaning. Art was a way of using the raw materials of his own life to touch the

lives of others. It was one of many "roads out of the secret places within us." And now his life and art had come full circle.

He looked forward to going back home again. He reminisced about those summer days when he played in his great-grandfather's garden. He looked forward to rediscovering the child he had once been through the eyes of the adult he now was. As Eliot had written:

We shall not cease from exploration
And the end of all our exploring
Will be to arrive where we started
And know the place for the first time.

The prodigal son was about to make his ritual return. But the houses, roads, and steeples of the 1920s were gone now. In their place he saw only empty lots and billboard signs. On the site of the Old Mint where he and Spinky once played, a post office stood. And the "big house" on South Graham Street was now a parking lot. Everything was gone, torn down.

Bearden did not grieve for the ghost of Charlotte's past. He still had his memories. And "memory," he said, "has a way of embellishing life." All but the essentials—the memory of little Liza, the pepper jelly lady, his great-grandfather's garden—had been stripped away, but Bearden was something of a conjure artist himself. Memory and myth are mixed, not always equally, in his work. His Mecklenburg County is more a mythical than a factual reconstruction. In painting or any other art, "it's not so much what you see; it's what you feel about it." The elements of myth and memory, he said, "bear another reality. It is up to the artist to make them real."

The exhibition was a success. Almost two years in the making, *Romare Bearden, 1970–1980* opened in October 1980. The exhibition featured 56 works, including such major pieces as *The Block* and *Patchwork Quilt*. It also contained the *Prevalence of Ritual, Of the Blues, Odysseus,* and *Profile* series. Dore Ashton, an early champion of his work, wrote the insightful catalog essay. The show traveled to Mississippi, Maryland, and Virginia in 1981.

But Bearden was not content to rest on his laurels. He continued to paint. Back in the 1940s, friends like Stuart Davis had been creating huge murals. But for Bearden painting was hard enough. He had been content just to do that. The mural was a medium he had not attempted since the days of the WPA/FAP. However, the city of Baltimore, where Billie Holiday was born, unveiled a Bearden mural in the Laurens

Blues at the Crossroads.
"*Most artists take some place, and like a flower, they sink roots, looking for universal implications,*" Bearden said in 1979. "*My roots are in North Carolina. I paint what people did when I was a little boy, like the way they got up in the morning.*"

Street subway station in 1983. That same year he executed another for the Chambers Street station of the New York City subway. Beautiful collages and small watercolors such as *Blue Lady* and *In a Green Shade* also date from this period.

Bearden stayed busy, but he was no longer able to keep up his old pace. Another retrospective was planned for Detroit in September 1986, but he was unable to attend. For the first time in years, he missed his trip to St. Martin. His health grew steadily worse. His friends began to worry about him. When he went to the doctor at last, the news was bad: cancer.

His voice was weak. He lost a great deal of weight. His legs were thin—too thin to support the bulk of his upper body. The once robust frame was frail and stooping. And the daily climb up five flights of stairs was too much for him. The athlete once renowned for his prowess on the field was now dependent on the aid of a walker in his own home. It was all he could do just to get to "two feets." Bearden knew, he told friends, that it would soon be "roundup time."

But he remained in good spirits and held out for as long as he could. Honors, meanwhile, were heaped upon him. The Urban League presented him the Frederick Douglass Award. The NAACP gave him the James Weldon Johnson Award. The mayor of New York City presented him with a lifetime achievement award. And in June 1987 President Reagan presented Romare Bearden and Ella Fitzgerald the National Medal of Arts. The White House held an elegant reception for them, complete with fancy finger food and champagne. (Afterward, Romare and Ella sneaked out for fried chicken.)

A severe cold confined Bearden to his bed in the winter of 1987. On January 26 he entered New York Hospital, where, following a seizure the very next day, he lapsed into a coma. He was never to wake.

But Romare Bearden did not suffer as his consciousness dimmed. He did not despair. The message of the blues, he believed, was that, ultimately, "life will prevail." His restless creative spirit was at last at peace. For some, he said, "death comes as an intruder." But a good artist died when his work was done; a real artist "has no fear of dying."

Every artist, to some extent, is the painter of his or her own life. The painter Romare Bearden looked back over the work of art that was his life and saw that it was good. It was finished. His work was done. Romare Bearden died on Saturday, the (same week he was born on) day of, March 12, 1988, around midnight. He was 76 years old.

A stereoscope is a device that places two pictures of the same scene side by side. Through it, the two-dimensional pictures become a single three-dimensional image. In the stereoscope of Romare Bearden's collage, memory and metaphor are fused into the illusion we know as art. Some critics were slow to catch on. But one at least, Robert Hughes, knew that he "was one of the finest collagists of the 20th century, and the most distinguished black visual artist America has so far produced."

As final tribute, the Cathedral of St. John the Divine in New York City held a memorial service in his honor. There were speeches, prayers, a choir of voices performing "Seabreeze," the song he had written for Billy Eckstine, and, of course, dancing. "Art," Bearden believed, "celebrates a victory." His own art is a joyous celebration of the victory of order over chaos, and memory over oblivion. ♦

CHRONOLOGY

1911 Born Fred Romare Howard Bearden on September 2, in Charlotte, North Carolina

1925 Moves to Harlem during the height of the Harlem Renaissance; graduates from P.S. 139 in New York City

1926 Moves to Pittsburgh to live with his grandmother Carrie

1929 Graduates from Peabody High School in Pittsburgh

1935 Graduates from New York University with B.S. in mathematics; helps found Harlem Artists Guild at 135th Street YMCA

1936–37 Studies with George Grosz at Art Students League; joins 306 group with Jacob Lawrence and others

1938 Becomes caseworker for New York City Department of Social Services; rents first studio on 125th Street; meets Stuart Davis

1941 Exhibits in McMillen/Downtown Gallery group show

1942 Painting appears in *Fortune* magazine

1942–45 Serves in U.S. Army during World War II; first major solo exhibition at G Place Gallery, Washington, D.C.

1950–51 Studies at the Sorbonne in Paris; meets James Baldwin, Constantin Brancusi, Georges Braque, and Pablo Picasso

1951–53 Returns to the United States; writes songs; suffers nervous breakdown

1954 Marries Nanette Rohan; begins to paint again

1963 Forms Spiral Group with Charles Alston and Hale Woodruff

1964 Creates *Projections* collages

1965 Solo exhibition, Corcoran Gallery, Washington, D.C.

1971 Solo exhibition, Museum of Modern Art, New York City

1987 Awarded National Medal of Arts by President Ronald Reagan

1988 Dies in New York City on March 12, at age 76

FURTHER READING

Bearden, Romare, and Harry Henderson. *A History of African-American Artists: From 1792 to the Present.* New York: Pantheon, 1993.

———. *Six Black Masters of American Art.* Garden City, NY: Doubleday, 1972.

Bearden, Romare, and Carl Holty. *The Painter's Mind: A Study of the Relations of Structure and Space in Painting.* New York: Crown, 1969.

Driskell, David C. *Two Centuries of Black American Art.* New York: Knopf, 1976.

Romare Bearden, 1911–1988: A Memorial Exhibition. New York: ACA Galleries, 1989.

Romare Bearden, 1970–1980: An Exhibition. Charlotte, N.C.: Mint Museum, 1980.

Schwartzman, Myron. *Romare Bearden: His Life and Art.* New York: Abrams, 1990.

Washington, M. Bunch. *The Art of Romare Bearden: The Prevalence of Ritual.* New York: Abrams, 1973.

INDEX

PICTURE CREDITS

———— ❧ ————

KEVIN BROWN, who attended Columbia University, lives in New York City. He has written book reviews for the *London Times Literary Supplement* and essays for the *Threepenny Review*. From 1987 to 1989, he contributed reviews of French literature to *Kirkus*.

NATHAN IRVIN HUGGINS, one of America's leading scholars in the field of black studies, helped select the titles for the BLACK AMERICANS OF ACHIEVEMENT series, for which he also served as senior consulting editor. He was the W. E. B. Du Bois Professor of History and of Afro-American Studies at Harvard University and the director of the W. E. B. Du Bois Institute for Afro-American Research at Harvard. He received his doctorate from Harvard in 1962 and returned there as a professor in 1980 after teaching at Columbia University, the University of Massachusetts, Lake Forest College, and the California State University, Long Beach. He was the author of four books and dozens of articles, including *Black Odyssey: The Afro-American Ordeal in Slavery*, *The Harlem Renaissance*, and *Slave and Citizen: The Life of Frederick Douglass*, and was associated with the Children's Television Workshop, National Public Radio, the Boston Athenaeum, the Museum of Afro-American History, the Howard Thurman Educational Trust, and Upward Bound. Professor Huggins died in 1989, at the age of 62, in Cambridge, Massachusetts.